Alicia Alonso
Dances On

Rose Viña   illustrated by Gloria Félix

Albert Whitman & Company
Chicago, Illinois

To the Viña family—especially my grandfather, Carlos Viña,
who taught us all to keep a song in our heart—RV

To my parents, and to Francisco for always being there for me—GF

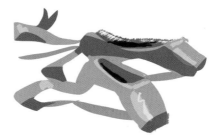

Library of Congress Cataloging-in-Publication data
is on file with the publisher.

Text copyright © 2021 by Rose Viña
Illustrations copyright © 2021 by Albert Whitman & Company
Illustrations by Gloria Félix
First published in the United States of America
in 2021 by Albert Whitman & Company
ISBN 978-0-8075-1454-2 (hardcover)
ISBN 978-0-8075-1456-6 (ebook)

Printed in China
10 9 8 7 6 5 4 3 2 1 WKT 26 25 24 23 22 21

Design by Valerie Hernández

For more information about Albert Whitman & Company,
visit our website at www.albertwhitman.com.

Cuba, 1929

Alicia whirls around cars and leaps over puddles as she twirls through the colorful neighborhoods of Havana.

She's excited to attend her first clase de baile.

Pro-Arte Musical is the only place to offer ballet classes on the island!

Alicia practices all the ballet moves:

plié,

relevé,

arabesque.

The studio has little money, and every student practices in their tennis shoes.

Alicia doesn't mind; she just wants to learn new moves!

Alicia grips the barre as she rolls up onto the balls of her feet.

Up and down.

Down and up.

Again and again, hundreds of times.

Her feet dance, her legs dance, and her arms dance, too, as she sways to the música, feeling it deep inside.

One day her teacher brings in pointe shoes—the only pair
available in the country.

All the students try them on, but they don't fit. Alicia touches the
silky ribbons and smooth sides. She slips them on. Perfecto!

Alicia watches as her reflection in the mirror
transforms into a ballerina.

But pointe shoes hurt. She wraps her feet in bandages and tries to ignore the pain as she breaks in the toe box.

Still, Alicia insists on wearing them everywhere. She only takes them off at night to tuck under her pillow.

While her friends dance the rumba under the warm summer sun, Alicia trains every day in the hot Havana studio. Her muscles and feet are sore, but she loves to dance more than anything in the world.

However, Alicia has learned all she can from her teacher. To become a professional ballerina, Alicia must leave her home behind.

Her father disapproves. He thinks dancing is not a real career.

Alicia packs her bags and says a tearful adiós to her family and friends.

New York City, 1937

On the busy streets, Alicia weaves in and out of crowds.
   The hustle and bustle is nothing like how it was in her
homeland, but Alicia can still feel the beat of Cuban songs
inside her heart.

Her classmates at the American Ballet Theatre show off their precise techniques, polished shoes, and pretty new tutus. Alicia keeps to herself. She doesn't understand all the inglés the teachers say, but she doesn't give up.

Alicia strikes a powerful pirouette while other girls delicately lift their arms. She hopes to stand out.

But some teachers are not impressed. One choreographer is especially strict and pushes Alicia and her classmates too hard.

Alicia stands up for herself and says to him, "You can't ever make me cry."

All the training begins to pay off.

Alicia flows from movement to movement, holding her head up.

She dances with her whole body.

"What beautiful lines she has!"

"Look at how perfect her technique is!"

But one day the sparkling theater lights start to dim.
She can't see the doors to the side, or make out her pink
pointe shoes below her. Alicia bumps into others and has trouble
balancing while turning. The other dancers whirl past her in
blurs of gray. A curtain-like shadow casts over her eyes.

"Cuidado! Watch out!" her partner yells as he catches Alicia.
Alicia blinks and squints, but the world around her is fading fast.

The doctor in New York has bad news: "You have an eye condition that's destroying your sight."

Desperate, Alicia has two surgeries. Each time she must stay in bed for months while her eyes heal. She fantasizes about lacing up her pointe shoes and wearing her favorite tutu.

When the surgeries don't work, Alicia decides to return to Cuba.
This time the doctors tell her to rest, or else she will go blind.
The songs in her heart begin to fade. How can she reach her
dreams now?

Alicia vows not to give up. She has another surgery. This time, she must stay in bed for a year.

In the darkness of her bedroom, Alicia softly moves her hands, lifting and twirling her fingers. She imitates the movements of the famous ballet *Giselle*. Alicia finds new inspiration from its story about a girl with a weak heart who doesn't want to give up dancing.

Alicia listens to ballet music, memorizing every beat, every note. She moves in her imagination with ease. The music inside starts to grow again as she waits for her chance to dance.

One year later, doctors remove the bandages. Alicia's family helps lift her out de la cama. Her muscles have lost their power. She must learn to walk again.

Alicia puts on her practice clothing and laces up her pointe shoes. She squints at her image in the mirror. Her eyesight is not perfect, but that doesn't stop her.

She returns to New York City.

Alicia trains día y noche. Her feet ache and bleed from the hard work.

At last she lands the leading role in *Giselle*.

Before the show, Alicia asks for help. Extra-bright spotlights shine near the edge of the stage, and a wire prevents her from falling into the crowd. Dance partners guide her carefully.

As she steps from the curtains, Alicia relies on her other senses. She feels the warmth of the spotlights glide over her and follows the music leading her across the stage. She takes a deep breath and allows the character, Giselle, to take over.

Alicia learns to dance through the darkness.

Directors around the world want Alicia to star in their productions. As a beautiful swan in *Swan Lake*, or a powerful woman in *Don Quixote*, Alicia connects with the characters she portrays.

She admires a blurry Eiffel Tower in Paris, and the edges of Saint Basil's Cathedral in Moscow.

Although the world is out of focus, Alicia Alonso's dream has never been clearer. Finally, she is a bailarina principal.

Cuba, 1958

Returning home to Havana, Alicia feels the familiar gravel beneath her and smells the blossoming mariposas in the air.

"Maybe other Cuban children wish to dance?" Alicia wonders.
She travels from village to village looking for children interested
in dancing.

Alicia takes to the stage, but in a new role—the director of the Ballet Nacional de Cuba. She smiles as she hears children tip-tap their excited feet into the studio, eager to start their first class.

Alicia shows her estudiantes how to stretch in their leaps
and pirouette with straight backs. She teaches them how to be
graceful and strong with each movement.

She also teaches them to follow the songs in their hearts—
just like her.

Alicia Ernestina de la Caridad del Cobre Martínez y del Hoyo was born in Havana, Cuba, in 1920. At the age of five, Alicia would dance with long scarves while her mother played music on a phonograph. Three years later her mother signed Alicia up for her first dance class.

The dance school had very little money and only one teacher. By the time Alicia was sixteen, she knew she had to venture to New York City to advance her career. Her father greatly disapproved, exclaiming that "ballet was not a real career."

However, the move proved to be successful, and Alicia's dancing abilities grew, as did her love for fellow Cuban dancer, Fernando Alonso. They married and had a daughter while living in the United States.

Soon after, Alicia's eyes started to deteriorate because the retinas were detaching. She became partially blind, and no surgery ever fully fixed the problem. But that never stopped her from doing what she loved. She trained hours and hours every day and eventually earned the starring role in the famous ballet *Giselle*. Many biographers and dance experts consider Alicia's role in *Giselle* to be her breakthrough performance.

Eventually she became a prima ballerina performing in countries as far away as Japan and Russia. Alicia's performances earned her dozens of top awards and the title prima ballerina assoluta, of which there are currently only thirteen in history.

When she wasn't traveling, Alicia divided her time between New York City and Cuba. However, Alicia chose to finish her career in Cuba, where her family still lives to this day. The dance school that she started eventually became Ballet Nacional de Cuba.

In 1999 Alicia was awarded the Pablo Picasso Medal by UNESCO. She was given four different honorary degrees, from multiple universities. She also received the highest civilian honors from the Dominican Republic, Mexico, and Panama, among others.

Alicia danced her last role when she was seventy-five years old, as a butterfly in a show she created called "Farfalla." She passed away in 2019 at the age of 98.

Resources

Arnold, Sandra. *Alicia Alonso: First Lady of the Ballet*. New York: Walker, 1993.

Bernier-Grand, Carmen T., illustrated by Raúl Colón. *Alicia Alonso: Prima Ballerina*. Tarrytown, NY: Marshall Cavendish, 2011.

Siegel, Beatrice. *Alicia Alonso, the Story of a Ballerina*. New York: Frederick Warne, 1979.

Simón, Pedro, dir. *Alicia Alonso: Prima Ballerina Assoluta*. Pleasantville, NY: Video Artists